OPRAH WINFREY

DISCOVER THE LIFE OF AN AMERICAN LEGEND

Don McLeese

Rourke
Publishing LLC
Vero Beach, Florida 32964

www.rourkepublishing.com

PHOTO CREDITS: © Paul Natkin/Photo Reserve

Cover: *Oprah shows her famous smile.*

Editor: Frank Sloan

Cover design by Nicola Stratford

Library of Congress Cataloging-in-Publication Data

McLeese, Don.
    Oprah Winfrey / Don McLeese.
        p. cm. — (Discover the life of an American legend)
    Summary: A simple biography of Oprah Winfrey, who overcame her difficult
    childhood to win success as a talk-show star, actress, and role model.
    Includes bibliographical references and index.
    ISBN 1-58952-306-7
    1. Winfrey, Oprah—Juvenile literature. 2. Television personalities—United
    States—Biography—Juvenile literature. 3. Actors—United States—
Biography—Juvenile literature. [1. Winfrey, Oprah. 2. Television personalities. 3.
Actors and actresses. 4. Women—Biography. 5. African Americans—Biography.]
I. Title. II. Discover the life of an American Legend (Vero Beach, Fla.)

PN1992.4.W56 M39 2002
791.45'092—dc21
[B]   2002069805

Printed in the USA

w/w

TABLE OF CONTENTS

QUEEN OF ENTERTAINMENT

Oprah Winfrey is one of the most famous stars on **television**. Some say she is also the most powerful woman in the history of American **entertainment**. Her program, "The Oprah Winfrey Show," is the most popular television talk show ever.

Oprah has acted in and produced movies. Her magazine has become a big hit. It is called "O, The Oprah Magazine." The Oprah Book Club on her TV show turned every book she chose into a bestseller. Her Angel Network has given away millions of dollars to people who are trying to do good. Wherever she turns, Oprah has made a big difference in a lot of people's lives.

Stars like Cher appear on Oprah's show.

BORN POOR

Oprah Gail Winfrey was born on January 29, 1954, in Kosciusko, Mississippi. Her parents, Vernita Lee and Vernon Winfrey, were poor teenagers. They weren't even married. They wanted to name their daughter "Orpah," after a person in the Bible. Somehow the name was not spelled right, and she became "Oprah." No one ever had that name before!

Her parents wanted to name her "Orpah."

MOVED AROUND

Oprah's parents didn't live together, so their daughter lived in different homes. She spent her early childhood on her grandmother's farm. She then moved to Milwaukee to be with her mother. She got into a lot of trouble in her early teens. Her mother threatened to send her to a home for troubled girls.

Now a happy adult, Oprah had
a troubled childhood.

STRAIGHTENING UP

Instead, Oprah went to live with her father in Nashville, Tennessee. He was a **barber** and businessman. He knew he had to be really strict to keep Oprah out of trouble. He told her how important school was, and he didn't let her run wild. Oprah turned her life around while living with her dad.

LOCAL STAR

When she was still in high school, Oprah got her start with a radio program. She won the Miss Black Tennessee contest in 1971. Then she became a TV **newswoman** in Nashville. She was so popular that a Baltimore TV station hired her for her first talk show.

Oprah was a beauty queen.

GOING NATIONAL

Oprah became a national star after moving to Chicago in 1984. Her program was renamed "The Oprah Winfrey Show." It soon became the most popular talk show in television history. People loved Oprah because they felt she understood their hopes and problems. She was just like them!

Oprah's popular talk show

BEYOND TELEVISION

In 1985, Oprah was asked to appear in a movie called *The Color Purple*. She was so good that she was nominated for an **Academy Award**. She made more movies as an **actress** and produced them for TV. She became one of the richest and most powerful women in America.

Dolly Parton makes music with Oprah.

AMERICA'S CINDERELLA

Oprah's life has been almost like a fairy tale. She was a poor girl with a tough childhood. But she became the **queen** of all entertainment!

One of the country's most admired people

Both Oprah's magazine and book club show that millions of **fans** trust her. They also love her. As successful as Oprah is, she still seems to care about people.

GLOSSARY

Academy Award (uh CAD uh me uh WARD) — a top award for a movie, also called an "Oscar."

actress (ACK trus) — a female actor.

barber (BAR bur) — someone who cuts hair

entertainment (en tur TAYN ment) — something you watch or do for fun

fans (FANZ) — people who admire someone or something

newswoman (NEWS wuh mun) — someone who reports the news on TV or in a newspaper.

queen (KWEEN) — female ruler

television (TEL uh vizh un) — shows programs for home entertainment, TV

INDEX

Further Reading

Frederich, Belinda. *Oprah Winfrey*. Chelsea House Publishers, 2001.

Krohn, Katherine E. *Oprah Winfrey*. The Lerner Publishing Group, 2001.

Stone, Tanya Lee. *Oprah Winfrey: Success with an Open Heart*. Millbrook Press, 2001.

Websites To Visit

http://www.oprah.com

http://www.davison.k12.mi.us/dms/projects/women/awinfrey.htm

http://www.achievement.org/autodoc/page/win0bio-1

About The Author

Don McLeese is an award-winning journalist whose work has appeared in many newspapers and magazines. He is a frequent contributor to the World Book Encyclopedia. He and his wife, Maria, have two daughters and live in West Des Moines, Iowa.